THE ALPHABET
OF CREATION

An ancient legend from the Zohar

with drawings by BEN SHAHN

SCHOCKEN BOOKS · NEW YORK

Adapted from *The Jewish Anthology*, edited by Edmond Fleg and
translated by Maurice Samuel, by permission of the publishers,
Behrman House, Inc. 1261 Broadway, New York, New York.

Twenty-six generations before

the creation of the world, the

twenty-two letters of the alphabet

descended from the crown of

God whereon they were engraved

with a pen of flaming fire. They

gathered around about God

and one after another spoke and

entreated, each one, that the world

be created through him.

The first to step forward was

Tav. "O Lord of the World,"

said he, "be it Thy will to

create the world through me,

seeing that it is through me that
Thou wilt give the Torah to Israel
by way of the hand of Moses. For
it is written: 'Moses commanded
us to keep the Torah.'"

The Holy One, blessed be He,
made answer and said, "No . . .

Because in the days to come I shall place thee as a sign of death upon the foreheads of men." And Tav retired.

Shin then stepped forward. "O Lord of the World, create Thy world through me, seeing that

Thine own name, Shaddai, begins

with me!" But Shin was rejected

because it was his ill fortune to

stand at the beginning of the words

Shav, lie, and Sheker, falsehood.

So it was with Resh that stands

at the head of Ra, wicked, and

Rasha, evil, even though he could

claim the honor of being the first

letter in the name of God —

Rahum, the Merciful.

Koph, in his turn, had to be
rejected, for although he begins the
word Kodesh, the Holy One, he
also suffers himself to be used for
the word curse — Kelalah.

When the letter Zadhe presented

himself, saying that he stood at

the head of the word Zaddik, the

Righteous One, God replied, "O

letter Zadhe, you are good and you

are true, but it is you that will

stand for Zarot, the misfortunes of

Israel!" And Zadhe went away.

Next came Pe that claimed the word Podeh, the Redeemer, to his credit. But God said, "You have the lowered head, symbol of the sinner who, ashamed, lowers his head and covers it with his arm. Besides, Peshah, transgres-

sion, reflects dishonor upon the

letter Pe."

The letter Ayin presented himself,

showing that it was with him that

the word Anawah, humility, began.

But the Lord, blessed be He, said

unto him: "I cannot use you for

the beginning of the world, for it

is with you that the word Aerwah,

immorality, begins."

And when the Ayin had left,

Samekh entered saying: "O Lord,

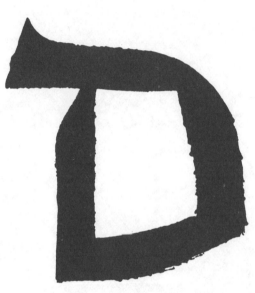

be it Thy divine will to create the

world through me, seeing that

Thou art called Samekh after me,

the Upholder of all that fall!"

But God said, "Remain, Samekh, where you are. For you must continue to uphold all that fall."

Nun, although he introduces Ner,

"the lamp of the Lord which is the

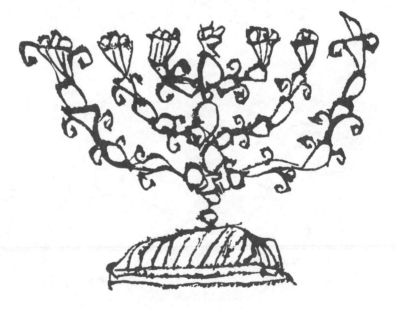

spirit of men," equally introduces

Ner, "the lamp of the wicked

which will be put out by God."

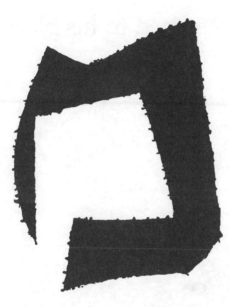

And as for Mem, "It is true," the

Lord said, "that you serve Me by

starting the word Melek, king,

which is one of the titles of God,

but you are also the first letter

of Mehumah, confusion." So the

Mem returned to his place.

Lamedh now came forward, boldly

proclaiming himself to be the first

letter of Luhot, the celestial tables

on which would be inscribed the

Ten Commandments. But he had

failed to remember that the tables

would be shattered by Moses.

At this moment the letter Khaph

descended from the glorious crown

and cried out, "Master of the

Universe! May it please Thee to

use me for the creation of the

world. For it is known that Kisseh,

the throne of God, as well as

Kabod, his honor, and Keter, his

crown, all begin with me!" And

the Lord, blessed be He, said,

"I will smite together my hands,

Khaph, in despair over the mis-

fortunes of Israel!"

Yodh then entered and asked to be

chosen, for did he not form the

first letter of the sacred name of

God—Yah? But then it was pointed

out that Yezer ha-Ra, the evil

inclination, begins also with Yodh.

Teth based his claim upon being the

initial letter of Tov, the good, which

is one of the attributes of God.

But God spoke to him saying,

"The truly good is not in this world,

it belongs in the world to come."

Heth, although it is the first letter

of Hanun, the Gracious One, is also

first in the word for sin — Hattat.

So the letter Heth was rejected.

Zayin based his plea upon the fact

that he begins the verse which

ordains the observance of the

Sabbath. But God said, "You may

not help Me in the work of the

creation of the world, for Zayin

is the word for weapon, which is

the image of war."

The letters Vau and He entered

together saying, "O Lord, create

the world through us, for together

we compose the ineffable name of

God." But God replied, "You are

too exalted for use in the affairs of

the world." So they returned to

their places.

If Daleth had begun only the word

Dabar, the Divine Word, it might

have been used. But it stands also

at the head of Din, justice. And
under a law of justice without
love, the world would have fallen
to ruin.

Thus Daleth was disqualified.

And Gimel, although it reminds

one of Gadol, great, would not do,

because it also stands at the head

of Gemul – retribution.

When the letter Beth left the

crown, two hundred thousand

worlds, as well as the crown itself,

trembled. Beth stepped before the

Holy One, blessed be He, and

pleaded, "O Lord of the World!

May it be Thy will to create the

world through me, seeing that all

the dwellers in the world daily

give praise unto Thee through me.

For it is said, 'Baruch—blessed—be

the Lord forever: Amen and

Amen!'" The Holy One, blessed

be He, immediately granted the

petition of Beth, saying, "Blessed

be he that cometh in the name of

the Lord!" And He created the

world through Beth; as it is said,

"Bereshith—in the beginning—God

created the Heaven and the Earth."

The letter Aleph remained in her place. And the Lord, blessed be He, said to her, "O Aleph, Aleph, why have you not presented a claim before Me, as have the other letters?" Aleph replied, "Master of the Universe! Seeing that all these letters have presented themselves before Thee uselessly, why should I present myself also? And then, since I have seen Thee accord to the letter Beth this precious honor, I would not ask the Heavenly King to reclaim that which He has given to one of His servants."

The Lord, blessed be He, replied, "O Aleph, Aleph! Even though I have chosen the letter Beth to help

Me in the creation of the world,
you too shall be honored." And
God thereupon rewarded Aleph
for her modesty by giving her first
place in the Decalogue.

THE ALPHABET OF CREATION is one of the legends from the *Sefer Ha-Zohar,* or *Book of Splendor,* an ancient Gnostic work written in Aramaic by a thirteenth century Spanish scholar named Moses de Leon who presented the work, not as his own, but as mystic knowledge revealed many centuries earlier to the Rabbi Simeon Ben Yohai. The present interpretation has been rather freely adapted by Ben Shahn from the English translation of Maurice Samuel and other sources.

Conceived and illustrated by Ben Shahn, the original edition of this book, limited to 550 copies, was set in Emerson type.